20th Century

Farming

Graham Rickard

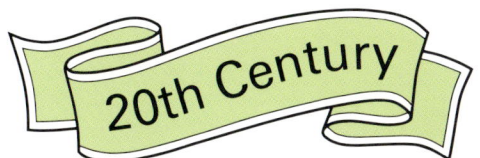

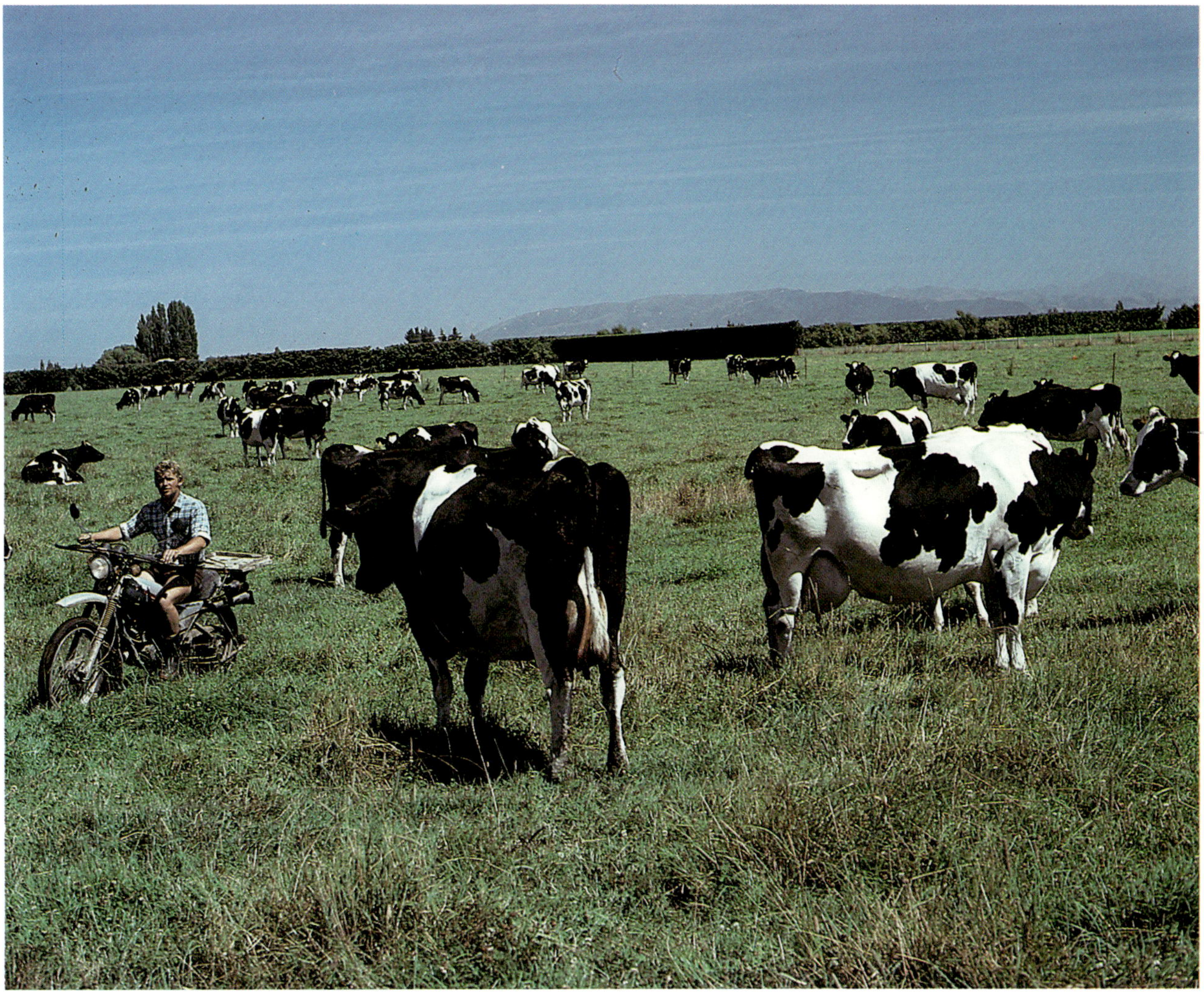

Wayland

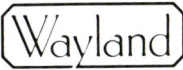

Titles in this series
**Art
Cinema
Communications
Fashion
Farming
Medicine
Transport
Warfare**

Editor: Francesca Motisi

Designer: Charles Harford HSD

Front cover, main picture *Harvesting barley in Germany.*
Front cover, inset *Ploughing in Buckinghamshire, Britain, 1922.*
Title page *The motor cycle is now more widely used than the horse on New Zealand's dairy farms.*
Back cover *Tractor and bullocks both used for ploughing, Badripur, India.*

First published in 1988 by
Wayland (Publishers) Ltd
61 Western Road, Hove
East Sussex BN3 1JD, England

© Copyright 1988 Wayland (Publishers) Ltd

British Library Cataloguing in Publication Data
Rickard, Graham
20th Century Farming.
1. Great Britain. Agricultural industries,
1900–1987
I. Title   II. Series
338.1′0941

ISBN 1-85078-925-7

Typeset by Kalligraphics Ltd, Horley, Surrey, England
Printed by G. Canale and C.S.p.A., Turin, Italy
Bound in by Casterman, S.A., Belgium

Contents

1900–1918 The Beginnings of Modern Agriculture

From muscles to machines	4
Colonial agriculture	5
Mechanization	6
The First World War	7

1918–1939 Farming in Decline

War debts	8
Deep-freezing and other advances	9
The Depression	10
The New Deal and beyond	12

1939–1949 The Second World War and after

The devastation of war	14
The post-war years	16
The advance of science	19

1950–1960 The Growth of Agribusiness

Farming as an industry	20
The formation of the EEC	24

1960–1970 The Green Revolution

Modern methods	26
The developing world	28

1970–1980 Farming and the Environment

The results of modern farming	32
Industrial pollution and farming	37
A return to tradition	37

1980–1990 Glut and Famine

Feast or fast?	38
The progress of science	42

Glossary 46

Further Reading 47

Index 48

The Beginnings of Modern Agriculture

At the turn of the century, European farming was in decline, unable to compete with massive imports of cheap food from Europe's overseas colonies, and from the 'new' lands – North America, Australia and New Zealand.

Below In nineteenth-century Britain, mobile threshing machines were belt-powered by steam engines, and were towed from farm to farm.

Inset Sometimes old fashioned steam-threshing machines are still used today for demonstrations.

From muscles to machines

In 1900, 80 per cent of the world's population still worked on the land, compared with only 6 per cent who work on today's hi-tech farms. In the eighteenth and nineteenth centuries, farmers had already seen many improvements in agriculture, such as new breeds of plants and animals and the introduction of crop rotation and artificial fertilizers. Machines were used to produce more food to feed the ever-growing populations of the new cities, which grew up around the factories of the Industrial Revolution. Heavy steam tractors were sometimes used for ploughing and threshing, and there were horse-drawn machines for cutting and baling hay and straw. But farming was still very labour-intensive, with much of the energy supplied by human and animal muscle power, and most farm-produce was sold locally.

Above A horse-drawn reaper in Fosterfields, New Jersey (USA), used to harvest a crop of maize.

Left McCormick's Reaping Machine was pulled by horses, and its chain-driven blades could be used to harvest different cereals.

Colonial agriculture

Most European countries, including Britain, Holland and France, had foreign colonies in India, the West Indies and elsewhere. Europe dominated the world, and the whole of Africa had been carved up and divided between these European empires. Cheap local labour was used to work on large plantations, producing bananas, sugar, tea and coffee for the European market. As well as food, colonial agriculture also produced the raw materials for Europe's industries, such as cotton, palm oil, rubber and timber.

Mechanization

As new settlers moved westwards across North America, they ploughed up the vast prairies to grow corn. Both the farms and the fields were much larger than those in Europe, and were ideal for using new machinery. Some machines, such as the seed drill, had been developed in Britain in the nineteenth century, but were still pulled by horses or steam-engines until the invention of the tractor. In 1908, the American Henry Ford produced the first simple and efficient design, and he was soon manufacturing his Fordson tractors by the thousand. This new farm 'workhorse' greatly improved productivity, as farmers discovered that a man with a tractor could do three times as much work as a labourer with a team of horses. These new machines soon helped the farmers of the USA and Canada to produce an enormous surplus of cheap high-quality wheat, which was shipped to many parts of Europe.

In Australia and New Zealand, large sheep and cattle farms sold meat, wool, and dairy products to the British and European markets. The first refrigerated steamships made it possible for European housewives to buy cheap beef from Argentina, bacon from Denmark, and dairy produce from Holland. The invention of the tin-can, and improved transport by rail, road and canal made it much easier to distribute perishable foods over long distances.

European agriculture went into decline, as most farmers found it impossible to compete with this flood of cheap imported food. Many rural areas became almost deserted, as farm-workers were forced to leave their traditional way of life and find work in the factories of the new industrial towns.

Top right *A pioneering family in the USA take a rest on their long wagon-trail to Oregon.*

Right *Henry Ford owned many farms in the Dearborn area, Michigan, USA. Here he is trying out one of his 'automobile ploughs' – a 1908 prototype of his successful tractor design.*

The First World War

When the First World War broke out in 1914, many European governments soon realized that their policy of 'cheap food', at the expense of their own farming industries, had been short-sighted. As German U-boats started to attack convoys carrying essential food imports, severe food shortages caused rationing throughout Europe. In 1916, well over a million tonnes of merchant shipping was sunk. Throughout Europe, most able-bodied men had joined the army, and there was an acute shortage of manpower to work on the land. Much of the land was also ruined by the war; in France, for example, half of all the farming land was under bombardment, and useless for agriculture.

The British Government started an urgent programme to boost food-production, using 5,000 imported American tractors and volunteer labour, including schoolchildren and the Women's Land Army. Farmers were also guaranteed a fixed minimum price for many crops. These measures were very successful, and food output soared, saving Britain from defeat by starvation.

By the end of the war, 30 million people had been killed, and the land was laid waste wherever the fighting had taken place. Livestock had been killed, crops were ruined, and there was not enough manpower to repair the damage. The whole of Europe was plagued with economic problems and prices escalated as food remained scarce.

Above *During the First World War women worked hard on the land.*

Left *As troops shelter in their trenches, the surrounding countryside clearly shows the devastation caused by the First World War.*

1918–1939
Farming in Decline

In the inter-war years, farmers everywhere suffered badly from the worldwide economic depression, when prices dropped drastically and international trade came almost to a standstill.

Right Harry Ferguson sitting at one of his tractors, after ploughing and tilling a field in record time.

War debts

The countries of Europe had borrowed heavily from the USA to finance their war effort, and these crippling debts caused serious economic problems. As soon as peace came, the politicians forgot the lessons they had learnt during the war, and European farmers quickly lost their new-found prosperity. The return to a Free Trade policy, with no guaranteed minimum prices for farmers, led to a fresh flood of cheap imported food from overseas.

The large-scale use of artificial fertilizers started in the 1920s, as farmers tried to improve their productivity. Many factories were built throughout Europe to produce these new chemical fertilizers, but most farmers could no longer afford to buy them when food prices dropped during the following decade.

Deep-freezing and other advances

The technique of deep-freezing was discovered by the American, Clarence Birdseye in 1923, and this new way of keeping food fresh for a long time made it easier to transport farm produce over long distances. In the USA, in 1932, the first slatted pneumatic rubber tractor tyres were produced, which gave the tractor good grip in all conditions. In 1935, tractor design was revolutionized by Harry Ferguson, an Irishman who wanted to help the world by finding a simple way to produce more food. He perfected the 'three point lift', which enabled tractors to carry machines, rather than just towing them. He also fitted his tractors with this simple hydraulic system, worked by levers in the driver's cab, which could lift and lower farm implements and other heavy loads.

Great advances were made in dairy farming, including the introduction of high-yield Friesian cows. Productivity was further increased by a careful programme of selective breeding, using artificial insemination. Careful record-keeping was also used to improve the breed, and double the average output of each cow. All herds were tested for tuberculosis, and on dairy farms new standards of cleanliness were introduced. After the Second World War electric milking machines were used in the new milking-parlours, worked by a single operator, who could milk fifty cows an hour. Selective breeding was also applied to pigs, sheep, and chickens, to improve production of meat, eggs and wool.

In the 1930s, scientists in Holland and the USA discovered plant hormones, and found that they could be sprayed on fields to kill certain weeds, without damaging crops. Another plant extract, derris dust, was used as an effective insecticide, which was harmless to crops, livestock and humans (unlike the deadly arsenic which farmers had previously used). Experiments in plant-breeding produced new varieties of food plants. In 1924, Henry Wallace, an American farmer, developed 'Copper Cross', the first hybrid maize, which gave both a higher yield and increased resistance to disease. Within ten years, several new types of hybrid cereal seeds were being widely used throughout the United States.

Below *A worker checks the quality of a batch of seed at a factory producing hybrid maize seed.*

The Depression

In 1929, share prices on the USA Wall Street stock market dropped so disastrously that thousands of investors were made bankrupt overnight. The 'Wall Street Crash' affected industry, trade and agriculture all over the world, and started a long period of world-wide economic collapse, called the Depression. There was a world glut of food, but it could not reach the hungry millions because prices fell too low to pay the transport costs. Farmers burnt their crops and slaughtered the livestock which they could neither feed nor sell.

The prices of products like coffee and wheat fell disastrously, and Cuba's sugar exports dropped to a quarter of their previous value. Other agricultural countries, such as Poland, Brazil, Australia and Canada also suffered badly. Japanese farmers depended on rice and silk for their living, and when the price of both these products slumped, they named the 1930s 'the dark valley'. In Austria, citizens searched through refuse for something to eat, while farmers left their unsaleable crops to rot in the fields. Corn was used as a fuel, because it was cheaper than coal, and milk was poured away.

American farmers suffered very badly, and also had other disasters to face. In the Midwest, over-farming and a series of droughts in the 1930s reduced the topsoil to a sandy dust, which blew away in the wind, smothering crops and burying farmhouses. The 'Dust Bowl' covered an enormous area across west Kansas, Oklahoma, Texas, Colorado and New Mexico. Land which had once provided rich cereal harvests was turned into an arid and useless desert, and thousands of poverty-stricken families were forced to leave their farms.

Below *Crowds of investors outside the New York stock Exchange, during the worst 'crash' in the history of Wall Street.*

Above A deserted farmhouse in the dustbowl region of Texas, USA.

Left A farming family from Wisconsin (USA) kneels and prays for rain during the dustbowl era in the 1930s.

The New Deal and beyond

In 1934, President Roosevelt gave Americans some hope of recovery, when he announced his 'New Deal' – a package of economic reforms to help both industry and agriculture. Farmers were given loans to develop their farms and buy new machinery, and the government took over their previous debts from the banks. Work programmes helped the unemployed to find jobs in industry and on the land, and the American economy gradually recovered.

In Europe, some countries tried to protect their farmers by abandoning their Free Trade policy, and introducing protectionist measures, such as taxes and quotas on food imports. In Italy, for example, the fascist leader Benito Mussolini tried to make Italy self-sufficient by increasing food-production. The vast Pontine Marshes were drained and reclaimed as agricultural land, but his 'Battle for Wheat' did no more than scratch the surface of Italy's economic problems.

In Britain, farmers were offered subsidies to produce more sugar beet, cereals and beef. The 1931 Agricultural Act established Marketing Boards for certain produce, such as milk, potatoes, pigs, wool and eggs. All farmers sold their produce to the Board at a fixed price, rather than being forced to accept the low prices offered by merchants. The Agricultural Research Council was set up in the same year, to apply scientific methods to the testing of new farming techniques, and to find new plant and animal breeds. In spite of all these measures, British farmers still found it hard to make a living, and even more workers left their farms and villages for ever.

Below In Denver, Colorado, President Roosevelt defends the agricultural policies of his 'New Deal', which helped American farmers to survive and prosper after the Depression.

Left The King of Italy and Mussolini visit Castel Porziano near Rome in 1926, after waste ground had been turned into fertile fields.

Below After a bumper crop in 1947, peasant workers carry the grain from their collective farm to the mill, to be ground into flour.

Collective Farming in the USSR

The Russian Revolution of 1917 overthrew the monarchy and established the world's first communist state. In 1928, the Soviet leader Stalin introduced his Five Year Plan – a massive programme of industrialization to revive the failing Soviet economy. Agriculture in the USSR was also in a sorry state, with severe food shortages, and Stalin decided to force the farmers to increase productivity, to feed the industrial workers and to provide a grain surplus for export. He imposed a policy of collectivization, merging small family farms into larger units which could buy and make use of modern machinery. The better-off farmers – called 'kulaks' – tried to resist, and stuck to their old capitalist system of selling their food for profit, rather than accepting the low prices paid by the State. Stalin crushed them ruthlessly, and five million kulaks were either executed or left to die of starvation. Collectivization severely disrupted Soviet agriculture, and Stalin's insistence on exporting Soviet food to pay for foreign industrial machinery was largely to blame for the terrible famines of 1932–33.

The Second World War and after

During the 1940s, farmland all over the world was ruined by the ravages of war, and once again farmers were called upon to perform the impossible, by boosting their production to feed the armies and millions of starving civilians.

Right *German U-Boats attacked ships carrying food supplies.*

Below *American commandos under fire in 1944. Farmland was again devastated during the Second World War.*

The devastation of war

The Second World War was a much more global conflict than the First World War, and crops and farmland in many parts of the world were devastated. German submarines again attacked convoys of ships carrying food supplies to Europe, and food shortages and rationing soon became a way of life.

Left Cows destroyed by shellfire during the war. The bodies become bloated after death.

Below A member of the Women's Land Army during the Second World War.

Much of the European countryside again became a battlefield, especially in France, and many farmers found it impossible to carry on with their work. In Burma and the other countries of south-east Asia, the rice paddies were destroyed, and the civilian population was faced with starvation.

In Britain, the government started a crash programme of ploughing up unused grassland for growing more crops. The acute shortage of labour was overcome by using schoolchildren, prisoners-of-war and the 80,000 members of the Women's Land Army, who did every kind of work, from tractor-driving to rat-catching. Thousands of extra tractors were brought into use, and combine harvesters made their first appearance in British fields. New factories were set up to make tractors and farm machinery, as Britain became the most highly mechanized farming country in the world. Huge harvests resulted from this great national effort, producing just enough food for the country to survive.

The post-war years

After the war, when politicians began the task of rebuilding their exhausted and depopulated countries, farmers feared that the essential part which they had played in the war effort would again be forgotten. But, in Europe at least, the lesson had been learnt, and farmers were given official recognition and encouragement for the essential work which they do in providing food for the rest of modern industrial societies. The situation was so serious that countries which had recently been at war with each other had to join forces to help each other.

In the post-war years, most European governments finally realized how important it was to have a thriving farming industry to feed their rapidly growing populations, and they introduced effective new agricultural policies. In Britain, for example, the 1947 Agriculture Act was a great landmark in farming history, laying down the basic principle of guaranteed prices and markets for most important farm products. Farmers were given assurances about the security of their land, and an annual price review gave them the confidence to increase their productivity, by investing in new machinery and trying new farming methods. Grants encouraged them to improve their land with drainage and lime applications, and subsidies were given to those who kept cattle and sheep in difficult hilly areas. Horses almost disappeared from the countryside, as most farmers could finally afford to buy tractors.

Below One person's ration (for a week) of certain foods in post-war Britain.

Left New tractor-drawn machines, such as this baler made farm work quicker and easier.

Cloud Seeding

Plants and animals need water to survive, and drought is the main problem facing farmers in many parts of the world, especially in Africa and Asia. Shortly before the Second World War, the French meteorologist Bergeron invented his 'precipitation initiation process'. Using a high-flying aircraft, he dropped ice crystals into clouds, and the 'overloaded' clouds then dropped their moisture as rain. Unfortunately, this system only works on clouds which already contain ice crystals as well as water droplets.

In the late 1940s, the American V J Schaefer discovered that very small particles of 'dry ice' (frozen carbon dioxide) worked better than Bergeron's ice crystals. Another technique uses salt to form the water particles into larger drops, which then fall as rain.

In 1947, another American, B Vonnegut, found that silver iodide smoke can produce snowflakes in very cold clouds. Silver iodide is still used in modern research into cloud seeding, conducted mainly in Australia.

Right *In 1948, a Land Army girl sprays DDT powder on a field of seed potatoes in Kent, to protect the crop against Colorado beetles.*

DDT
In 1948, the Swiss chemist Paul Müller won the Nobel Prize for developing the first modern insecticide, DDT (dichlorophenyltrichloroethane). It was first used in Switzerland to control the Colorado potato beetle. It works by attacking the insect's central nervous system, and is effective against most insects. The Second World War gave the insecticide business an enormous boost, and DDT was widely used to protect troops against diseases.

However, many insects eventually became immune to DDT. It was found that DDT was accumulating in the tissues of insects and was passed on to other animals. Insect-eating birds were badly affected, and DDT was proved to cause cancer in humans. DDT is now banned in many countries as one of the worst and most long-lasting sources of environmental pollution. It has been replaced by safer modern insecticides.

The advance of science

Although the war was a time of great hardship for most people, it also speeded up the pace of scientific progress, and many new discoveries were made. The discovery of DDT, for example, provided the war-torn world with the first effective all-purpose insecticide, and was especially useful in Asia, where it was used against malaria-carrying mosquitoes. Harvesting cereal crops was a very time-consuming job, usually done by hand, until the development of the combine harvester, during the 1940s. The harvester, which at first was pulled by a tractor, greatly speeded up the work, by combining the operations of cutting the crop (reaping) and separating the grain (threshing). Combine harvesters soon became self-propelled, and the sight of large teams of men bringing in the harvest became a scene from the past.

The Food and Agriculture Organization (FAO) was formed in 1945, as a specialized agency of the United Nations. Its job is to co-ordinate international efforts to raise standards of agriculture and nutrition, and to improve the management of forests and other natural resources.

Above As part of a Food and Agriculture Organization (FAO) project in Turkey, women workers cultivate the soil in a field of tomatoes (1971).

Left Wheat is stacked in 'stooks' to dry, after being harvested by a reaping machine (1950).

1950–1960

The Growth of Agribusiness

As traditional family farming gave way to modern agribusiness, with its emphasis on efficiency, productivity and profits, farming became an industry rather than a way of life.

Farming as an industry

European governments were trying to rebuild their own economies in the difficult post-war years, and farmers were given more support than they had ever known in peacetime. Many foods were in short supply, and rationing was still common in the early years of the 1950s. As towns expanded into the countryside, farmers were under pressure to produce more food on less land, as cheaply as possible. Following the example of the USA, science and technology began to take over on the farm.

Modern intensive 'factory farming' methods were first applied to poultry farms. In Europe, chickens were still left to roam around the farmyard. But in the USA both 'broilers' (for eating) and 'layers' (for egg production) had been housed in large units

Right A team of combine harvesters cut the wheat crop in a huge open field in the USA.

Below A combine harvester cuts wheat in a large field in East Anglia, Britain.

Above Battery chickens never see daylight, and have very little space to move around in their tiny cages.

as early as 1920. In Britain, the farmer Geoffrey Sykes studied American methods and pioneered the broiler system, housing thousands of birds in large buildings. Later, laying hens were kept in cages in large battery houses, with trays to collect the eggs, and automatic systems to provide warmth, food and water. Cramped together, the birds might have died of disease without the new antibiotic drugs which were added to their food, as well as hormones to boost growth and egg-production. Factory farming greatly increased productivity, and reduced the price of eggs and chicken meat, which had previously been luxuries.

The new intensive methods were soon applied to nearly all types of farm animals. As an offshoot of its vast dairy industry, Holland pioneered the factory-farming of veal calves, using techniques which are now banned as being too cruel. Originally, the calves were kept in crates in total darkness, and regularly bled throughout their short lives, to produce the 'white veal' that was in popular demand. Using more scientific modern methods, the calves are now separated from their mother at birth, kept for twelve weeks in small separate pens and fed on a synthetic milk mixture to produce the white flesh.

Right *In Britain, wildlife suffered as hedgerows were removed, or replaced with wire-fences, which do not need as much maintenance.*

On the outskirts of towns and cities, the new 'market gardens' used acres of glasshouses to produce fruit, flowers and vegetables, in a pest-free artificial environment, where the heat, light and humidity were all automatically controlled. Encouraged by their governments, farmers invested in new machinery, buildings, fertilizers, and land improvement schemes. The introduction of new high-yield animal breeds, such as the Landrace pig, led to the near disappearance of many traditional breeds, along with horses, windmills, and armies of labourers in the fields. Even sheep were bred and reared according to public preference. Electric shearing clippers and chemical dips to control pests and parasites both helped sheep farmers to become more efficient and more profitable.

Hedges were destroyed, marshes drained, and trees removed to make room for the new machines, as both farms and fields became bigger. Farmers became businessmen, with their cost-efficiency and production figures carefully worked out. They also became increasingly dependent on the outside companies who supplied them with electricity, agrochemicals, fuel and animal feed.

Below *Large-scale tomato production is possible in horticultural greenhouses, where ideal growing conditions are automatically controlled.*

Left *These landrace piglets were bred to produce more meat more quickly than traditional breeds.*

Below *The swollen eyes show that this rabbit is suffering from myxomatosis.*

Myxomatosis

During the 1950s, Australia and Britain were troubled by a plague of rabbits, which damaged valuable crops and pastures. In one of the first attempts at biological pest control, both countries deliberately introduced the myxomatosis virus to their rabbit populations. The virus causes a deadly infectious disease in hares and rabbits, but does not affect humans or other animals. The countryside was soon strewn with millions of dead or dying rabbits, and the disease, although unpleasant, succeeded in bringing the rabbit population under control. Wild rabbits still carry the virus, but many seem to be developing an immunity to the disease.

The formation of the EEC

Having lost their former colonies, many European countries felt isolated, and found it difficult to cope in the new political climate. Previous enemies agreed to unite, in an attempt to make Europe into one single and independent world force. In 1957, France, Belgium, Italy, Luxembourg, the Netherlands, and West Germany signed the Treaty of Rome, and formed the European Economic Community (EEC, or Common Market). The aim of the EEC was to encourage economic co-operation and development, with a large degree of political unity. Import taxes and controls were abolished between member states, and a Common Customs Tariff was established for all goods imported from outside the Community. Agriculture in much of Europe was lagging

Below In the past the Common Agricultural Policy (CAP) has produced some problems like surpluses of grain. These grain 'mountains' have now been reduced as a result of the poor harvest in 1987.

behind that of other developed countries, and the Common Agricultural Policy (CAP) was introduced primarily to secure reasonably priced food. The CAP guarantees minimum prices by buying up certain food surpluses, gives farmers improvement grants to develop and modernize their farms, and offers them subsidies for growing certain crops or farming in difficult areas. These measures are paid for by the import duties which the Community imposes on food from other countries.

Britain initially refused to join the EEC, because the Commonwealth, which included Australia, New Zealand and Canada, provided a steady source of trade and food imports, but this was soon to change. Britain finally joined the EEC, along with Denmark, the Republic of Eire, Greece, Spain and Portugal, and the Community has since emerged as a significant world voice. The farmers of Australia and New Zealand, who had worried about the loss of their guaranteed British market, soon found new trading partners in Japan and south-east Asia. European farms, which had been under-mechanized and overmanned, soon became much more efficient, and the agricultural workforce was halved throughout the EEC. The CAP has produced some new problems, such as 'mountains' and 'lakes' of surplus food and wine, but in most countries it has played a major role in modernizing the agricultural industry.

Below *This Israeli family irrigated the desert to grow cotton on their kibbutz.*

Israel's Kibbutz system

In 1949, the state of Israel was established as a homeland for the world's Jews, who had suffered so badly during the Second World War. Much of the territory was arid and sandy scrubland, and had always been considered totally unsuitable for farming. Groups of people from all over the world joined forces to form collective communal farms, called kibbutzim. Within a few years, they had drained the malaria-infested marshes, and irrigated the dry semi-desert, and the kibbutzim became very successful agricultural units, using modern intensive methods. All the members of each kibbutz share the work and income equally, setting some money aside for future investment in new equipment and materials. The 250 kibbutzim use large amounts of organic fertilizer to produce fruit, cotton, vegetables, poultry and dairy products. Some also have fish farms, canneries, and refrigeration plants, as well as industrial workshops. Each kibbutz has its own school, medical system, laundry, shops and repair facilities, and large expensive machines are shared with other kibbutzim. Children start working six hours a week at the age of fourteen, and all cars and houses are communally owned. 4 per cent of Israel's population now live in kibbutzim, producing half the nation's food, and exporting 45 million dollars worth of produce every year. While people are leaving the countryside all over the rest of the world, the kibbutzim are so successful that they are attracting more and more people to join this unique way of life. However, some young Israelis are now leaving the kibbutzim to lead a different lifestyle.

1960–1970

The Green Revolution

In an attempt to help the starving millions in the world's underdeveloped countries, Western scientists and advisers tried to boost their food production by applying modern methods to the developing world's agriculture.

Modern methods

During the 1960s, scientists continued to find new food sources and farming methods. Mechanization gave way to automation and conveyor-belt production of eggs and meat. Soya beans were recognized as an important source of protein, and researchers found ways of making soya into a cheap substitute for meat. With more and more farming land being used for industry and housing, a new soil-less method of growing crops was tried out. Hydroponic cultivation involves growing plants by immersing their roots in a special solution, and was soon being used to grow glasshouse crops, such as tomatoes. Hydroponic methods need very little space or labour, and this technique is now used to grow indoor 'fields' of grass on trays, to feed cattle on intensive beef farms.

Below *An agricultural project for growing soya beans in Zaire.*

Left Tomatoes grown without soil using hydroponic methods in large modern greenhouses. The plants' roots are immersed in a solution of water and chemical nutrients.

The developing world

While farmers in the developed countries were making use of modern farming methods, most of the world's agriculture had remained unchanged for thousands of years. The overpopulated countries which most needed extra food depended on inefficient subsistence farming, and their local farmers could not afford to invest in the machinery and chemicals necessary to improve their output. Plagues of locusts and other pests, drought, floods and storms all made the farmers' lives even more difficult, and millions of people regularly died in the famines caused by these natural disasters.

During the 1960s, these nations were becoming even poorer, because their populations were rising incredibly fast, and there were less food and resources available. Agriculture was hampered by the overworking of exhausted soils, lack of education and training, and a severe shortage of money for improvement projects. Western medicine had helped to wipe out many killer diseases, but failed to find any new ways of

Below In Indonesia, bullocks are still used to plough the flooded paddy fields before planting rice.

feeding the increased population. Some Western experts decided to start a 'Green Revolution', by applying modern scientific methods to the agricultural problems of the world's underdeveloped countries, where starvation and malnutrition were rife. New tools and machines were tried, but made little impact in countries where fuel, spare parts and skilled labour were unobtainable. New types of high-yield varieties (HYV) of crops such as maize and short-stemmed wheat were introduced in Mexico, India, Pakistan, and Turkey, in an attempt to improve the food supply. Although production was increased in some places, the initial cost of the seeds was high, and the new crops needed a good supply of expensive artificial fertilizers. It was soon found that the new seeds had little resistance to disease or drought, and needed irrigation and pesticides to produce a good harvest. Because the plants were hybrids, new seeds had to be bought each year, rather than using part of the previous year's crop for seed. Some countries invested in the chemicals which they needed to thrive, but soon found themselves heavily in debt to foreign banks.

Above A small threshing machine speeds up the harvest of miracle rice in the Philippines during the Green Revolution.

Miracle rice

The International Rice Research Institute (IRRA) was founded in the Philippines in 1962, in an attempt to solve the severe world shortage of rice, which forms the staple diet of 60 per cent of the Earth's population. Research collected different samples of rice from all over the world, and their seed bank now contains the seeds of 45,000 different strains. Each variety has different qualities, and they were interbred to produce new rice varieties. A short-stemmed 'indica' rice from Taiwan was crossed with a tall strain from Indonesia, and the resulting plant was bred through five generations, to allow it to develop a resistance to disease and climate. The resulting strain, IR-18, was the first 'miracle rice'. Its yield was more than double that of traditional strains, and it matured very quickly. But it also had an enormous appetite for water and nitrogen, and needed to be well fertilized to achieve the best results.

Several other strains were soon developed, but consumers complained that the new rice tasted flat, and did not 'fluff up' properly when cooked. The increased harvests encouraged pests, and farmers could not afford the fertilizers and irrigation schemes which the crop needed. Nutritionists also claimed that the high-yield rice had less food value than the traditional fine-grain varieties.

Modern strains, such as the tastier IR-24, are being constantly developed, and future crops will hopefully be more nutritious. What is needed, though, is a programme of education, to persuade the rice-eating nations of South-east Asia to eat the healthier raw grains of 'brown' rice, rather than polished white rice, which is lacking in essential vitamins and minerals.

Right Mature seed heads of rice in the Hyderabad region of India.

Below Terraced rice paddies in Bali help to prevent soil erosion on the hillsides.

Rice is the world's most important food crop, and forms the basic diet of more than half the human race. In Asia's poorest and most heavily-populated countries, millions of families eat little else, and totally depend on the rice harvest for their survival. Scientists in the USA, the Philippines, Thailand and elsewhere turned their attention to this vital crop, and developed several new strains of 'miracle rice', which gave a higher yield than traditional varieties, with a shorter growing season and increased resistance to disease. The yield was further increased by the use of modern agrochemicals and machinery, but the farms in the 'Rice Bowl' countries of south-east Asia could not afford to use them. Many farmers were ignorant of the new developments, and were unwilling to change their centuries-old methods of cultivation.

Above Planting rice seedlings in paddy fields.

Those who tried the new strains of rice were not always pleased with the results. In spite of the bumper harvests, people in Thailand called it 'sticky rice', and found it lacking in taste and texture. Increased yields required increased labour, and often encouraged pests and diseases.

The United Nations Food and Agriculture Organization (FAO) and many other experts consider that the Green Revolution was a great success. Between 1966 and 1973, the area planted with new strains of wheat and rice expanded enormously, and the new varieties and farming methods did help to solve the food crisis in many countries. Colombia, for example, more than doubled its rice crop in ten years, and was able to harvest three crops a year with the new quicker-growing plants.

However, the well-meaning measures of the Green Revolution often produced the opposite of their intended effect, as rich farmers became richer, and the poorer ones were forced off the land to make way for large plantations of the new crops. People's diet suffered too, as traditional varieties of crops were replaced by single crops, which were often sold for export, rather than feeding the local population. India, for example, exports a million tonnes of wheat per year, but some people think that the farmers would be better employed growing fresh vegetables for their own people.

In general, the Green Revolution was not a success, because it tried to impose expensive Western technology and farming methods on agricultural systems which were not suited to them. The emphasis is now on finding low-cost ways of improving traditional methods and crops, such as sorghum and millet, which are more resistant to drought and disease.

Farming and the Environment

People in developed countries began to question the advantages of modern technology, when they realized how their industry and agriculture were seriously polluting the natural environment, and using up the earth's natural resources at an alarming rate.

The results of modern farming

In the 1970s, computers were first used on farms, and soon proved how helpful they could be for keeping accounts and records of crop yields and breeding programmes. New training schemes produced more educated farmers, and land-owners began to employ farm managers, who were more skilled with rulers and calculators than a plough.

Below Modern intensive farming relies on the use of selected chemical sprays to protect the crops from pests and disease.

During the decade, there was a great increase in the number of fish farms, providing a valuable source of cheap protein. Intensive fish farms were very successful in Japan, where farming land is scarce, and fish is a very important part of the national diet. Forestry also became an important industry, and vast plantations of conifers were established, to supply the growing market for timber and wood pulp. In Europe, the Common Agricultural Policy helped farmers to rapidly modernize their farms. The labour-force decreased, while productivity rose even higher: one farm-worker can now feed a hundred people.

Since the turn of the century, modern technology has allowed the agriculture and industries of the developed countries to supply the world with an ever-growing supply of cheap food and consumer goods. Western governments and banks encouraged farmers to invest in the latest machinery, chemicals and new farming techniques, to increase profits by growing more and more food. Few people ever spared a thought for the effects which this continual 'progress' was having on the countryside and its wildlife, and the earth's natural resources were carelessly exploited. The lessons of the past, such as the 'dust bowls' caused by poor farming in the USA and Australia, were ignored, and man-made poisons continued to pour into the ground, the atmosphere, and our oceans and rivers.

Left Ploughing has caused severe soil erosion in this area of California.

Below In New Zealand, helicopters are used to spray weed-killer over large areas of scrubland.

The ecology movement had begun in the 1960s, and started a growing public awareness of the dangers of pollution. International environmental groups, such as Greenpeace and Friends of the Earth, drew attention to the problem, and started to pressurize governments to impose stricter controls on all forms of pollution. Despite initial opposition, both farmers and politicians now recognize that maximum food production must be balanced against the conservation of our environment, if the human race and our planet are to survive.

Below 'Slash and burn' methods have destroyed this area of tropical rain forest in Bahia, Brazil, which was once the home of rare plants and materials.

One of the world's most valuable assets is its tropical rain forests, which produce enormous quantities of oxygen and atmospheric moisture, as well as providing a home for more varieties of animals and plants than any other habitat. Yet in Brazil alone, an area of rain forest as large as Britain will be destroyed in the next seven years, to make way for cattle ranches.

Soil erosion is also caused by ploughing up natural grasslands and overgrazing, as seen in the pastures surrounding the Sahara desert, which is now growing at the rate of 40 km every year. In the last ten years, productive land the size of the twelve countries of the EEC has been turned to dust. If the present pace of rain forest destruction continues, 40,000 different varieties of plants could become extinct in the next sixty years.

The environment is damaged by many other aspects of modern agriculture. Many wild animals and plants disappeared from the countryside, when farmers drained ponds, felled trees and destroyed hedgerows to make larger fields. Birds and butterflies are decimated by pesticides, which linger in insects's body tissues, and are passed along the food chain, contaminating both animals and humans. Weedkiller sprays drift across the countryside exterminating wild plants. Many fish die too, as nitrate fertilizers leach through the soil, poisoning the rivers which supply our drinking water. The meat produced on 'factory' farms often contains growth hormones and antibiotics, which can build up in our bodies to dangerous levels.

The Riches of the The Rain Forests

The subsistence farmers of underdeveloped nations are often forced from their land, and have to carve out new fields from the rain forests. Their 'slash and burn' methods damage the poor jungle soil, which can only grow one or two meagre crops before rain washes it into the rivers, and the farmers have to clear yet more land. Within twelve months of clearing the forest, all that remains is sand and stones, baked by the tropical sun.

An area of rain forest as large as Britain is destroyed every two years, and the irony is that it is all for nothing. Plants provide people with food, shelter, tools and medicine, but the qualities of only 1 per cent of jungle plants have so far been investigated. Even aspirin comes from willow bark, and modern surgery would be impossible without the muscle-relaxing drug tubocuraine, which is derived from the South American jungle plant curare. The plants of the rain forest are a vast 'gene bank', and many of them may some day be needed for cross-breeding with our food plants, to increase their resistance to disease. This happened in the last century, when a disease called 'blight' wiped out the Irish potato crop. The resulting famine left one million people dead and forced another million to emigrate. Plant breeders found a wild potato species in the South American Andes, and used it to produce new strains of blight-resistant potatoes. In the future, our survival may one day depend on genes from the plants of the rain forests – plants which are disappearing day by day, as we senselessly wreck our most precious resources.

Above After the rain forest has been cleared, the thin soil can only support one or two meagre subsistence crops before it is exhausted and reduced to dust.

Opposite The Sahara desert has advanced across the formerly fertile Sahal belt in Niger, Africa.

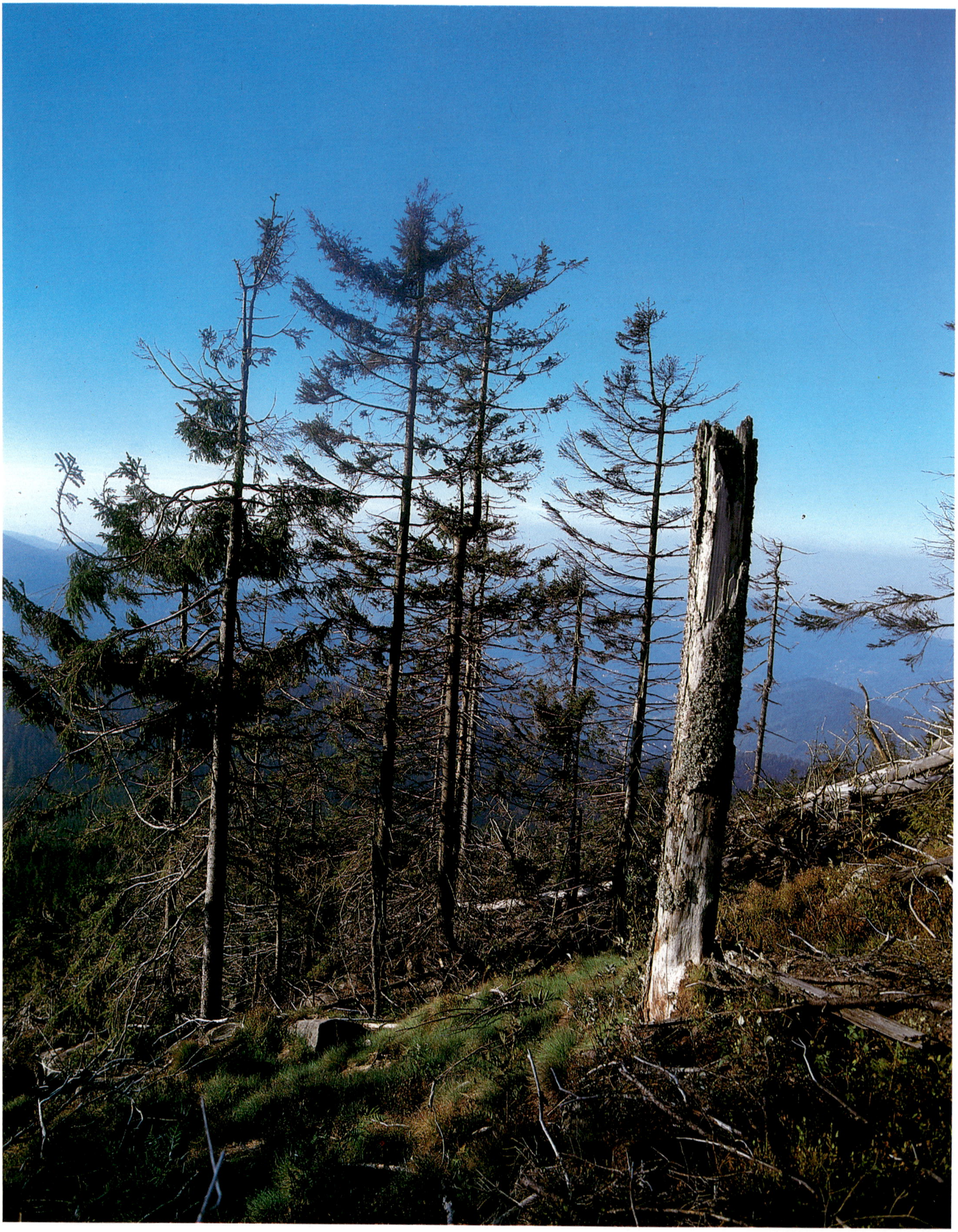

Industrial pollution and farming

Farming also suffers from industrial pollution. European coal-burning power stations emit large amounts of sulphuric acid. 'Acid rain' has ruined the forests and lakes of Scandinavian countries, which are now demanding much stricter controls on power station emissions. Nuclear power stations were once seen as a safe and clean alternative, but the explosion at Chernobyl in the USSR in 1986 clearly demonstrated the dangers of nuclear power. A large radioactive cloud passed over most of Europe, and the animals and crops of almost every country were affected. A large area of the USSR was evacuated, and now the land can never be farmed again. Contaminated milk and crops had to be thrown away, and the massive reindeer herds of Lappland had to be slaughtered. Some experts predict that flocks of sheep in parts of England and Wales will be affected by the disaster for the next thirty years.

Opposite *The effects of acid rain on the Black Forest in Germany.*

A return to tradition

The 1970s saw a great increase in the number of organic farmers, who were prepared to sacrifice a little productivity in the interests of environmental safety. Research in the USA has led to new methods of biological pest control. Organic crops, which sometimes may not look as attractive as those which have been treated with chemicals, need more labour to ensure a successful harvest; but what the organic farmer spends on extra wages, he saves on the costs of expensive chemicals. As the price of fuel and animal feed increased, stock farmers also began to turn their backs on modern methods, such as rearing animals in indoor factory farms. Pigs were once again turned loose in the fields, and many consumers were willing to pay more for free-range eggs, once they became aware of the conditions experienced by battery hens.

Above *This French farmer has turned his back on modern farming methods, and has returned to more natural 'organic' farming.*

1980–1990

Glut and Famine

While the richer developed nations produce more and more surpluses of unwanted food, most of the world still goes hungry because they cannot afford to pay for expensive food imports.

Feast or fast?

During this century, the rich nations have become richer and the poor ones have become poorer. Every hour, 400 people die somewhere in the world from starvation, or diseases caused by hunger. It is ironic that the world produces enough food to feed everyone. People are hungry because they no longer grow their own food, and cannot afford to buy it from others. They do not have the money to buy seeds, fertilizer and machinery, and their governments cannot help them. A wheat-farmer in the USA produces twenty-seven times as much food energy and forty-two times as much protein as a rice farmer in the Philippines, who still uses traditional agricultural techniques.

Below Contrast the farmer's speedy harvesting of wheat (Kansas, USA) with the slow and painstaking planting of rice in the Philippines (inset).

The developed industrial countries can afford to import large quantities of food, but poorer countries just do not have enough money. A quarter of the world's people, living in developed countries, eat more than half the world's food supply. Protein is essential in our diet, but the Western countries' demand for large quantities of meat worsens the world's food problems. Meat production is an inefficient way of using natural resources, and a piece of land can produce six times as much protein from plants as from grass-eating animals. Fish farming, yeasts, fungi and even algae are all being tested as possible future sources of protein-rich foods for humans.

Above On Japan's Shimo Peninsula, this seaweed farm has proved to be a valuable source of food.

In many underdeveloped countries, especially those which were once European colonies, the entire agricultural economy depends on one or two cash crops for export, such as bananas, cocoa or sugar-cane. These crops are at the mercy of disease, poor weather and falling market prices, and often do not leave enough land for the local population to grow food for themselves. Farmers are sometimes thrown off their land, so that their government can grow even more of these cash crops to repay their massive debts to Western banks. The natural environment is often damaged or destroyed in the drive to export more food.

During this decade, there have been worldwide food gluts and surpluses. In the EEC, production exceeded demand by four to one, and quotas have been introduced to make farmers keep their production down to strict limits. Many European farmers are in debt, and it is predicted that 10,000 farms will go out of business during the next few years.

India provides a good example of the twin problems of glut and hunger. Once the world's biggest receiver of foreign food aid, the Green Revolution has transformed the country's agriculture, and India is now an exporter of wheat – a situation which would have previously seemed impossible. India's granaries are overflowing with about 30 million tonnes of grain, yet 40 per cent of her people are still living below the poverty line. China has achieved self-sufficiency in grain, and in 1985 outstripped the USSR to become the world's largest wheat-producer. But Chinese authorities admit that about 90 million Chinese still do not have enough to eat.

Below Machine-harvesting sugar-cane in the Sudan.

Left Threshing and winnowing wheat by hand in China.

Below Many famous pop stars joined in the finale of the Live Aid concert in 1985. Nearly 80,000 people attended the concert.

Inset An exhausted Bob Geldof, with his wife Paula Yates, after masterminding the Live Aid concert to raise money for famine victims in Africa. This campaign raised millions of pounds to 'Feed the World', supplying food and long-term agricultural schemes to the refugees.

The progress of science

In spite of the world surplus of food, scientists continue to research new ways of boosting farm-production and efficiency still further. They are finding out more about the genetic codes that control growth and reproduction in plants and animals. The new science of biotechnology can alter the genetic make-up of plants to 'invent' new crop species, designed to resist pests and diseases, and produce enormous yields. Cloning techniques make it possible to use a few cells of a parent plant to produce thousands of identical copies, and animals are now bred by implanting foetuses in the womb. Irradiation techniques are now used in many countries to delay the decomposition of soft fruit and other perishable goods, and this could become a valuable new way of preserving food. Studies are being carried out to ensure that irradiation is not harmful.

Below *In a biotechnology laboratory, plant cells are given a small electrical current to stimulate their growth.*

Modern agriculture depends heavily on the use of pesticides, but these are losing their effectiveness, as pests develop an immunity. Weeds, too, have become resistant to herbicides, and many of these chemicals have been found to be dangerous to humans. A shortage of water and soil erosion are the biggest problems in many countries, where pastures and farmlands are rapidly turning into deserts. In many cases the lack of rainfall is a result of felling trees for timber.

Every year the world is losing 6 million hectares of farmland – an area the size of Belgium and the Netherlands combined – through soil erosion and new building. In the next decade, the world's population will exceed 6,000 million, and many problems will have to be overcome before we can distribute enough food to everyone.

Below In an American laboratory, a cylinder of fruit is subjected to X-rays to test the effects of irradiation on food.

Right Experimental work in agrigenetics showing young seedlings, developed from tissue cultures, and now growing in culture medium in test tubes. Tissue culture involves the growing of isolated plant cells, or a single cell, taken from almost any part of the parent plant. This technique enables prolific and rapid propagation and has been used to free crops of virus infection, since the virus does not penetrate certain tissue.

Opposite page This photograph is obviously posed but today's farmers are relying on computers more and more.

Computers on the farm
Computers are already being used in farm offices and milking parlours, and have proved to be a very useful tool in modern agriculture. Computers are used to keep detailed records of crop sowing dates, and the application of fertilizer and other chemicals. From his records, the farmer can check the progress of his crops, and work out the cost effectiveness of the chemicals which he uses. Calving dates, animal weights, milk yields, and market prices can all be carefully monitored, and the computer makes future financial planning much easier. Computers can also calculate economic mixtures of animal foodstuffs.

Some dairy cows now wear an electronic 'necklace', which gives out a radio signal. A computer in the milking parlour recognizes each cow by her signal, measures out exactly the right amount of food, and records her yield at each milking.

In the fields, other computers are used to monitor the operations and settings of combine harvesters and other complex machinery. Seed drills, for example, are now fitted with a microprocessor to calculate the right amount of seed to sow for different fields and crops.

Glossary

Agriculture The cultivation of the land to rear crops and livestock, for food, fuel and other uses.
Agrochemicals The chemicals used in modern farming, including fertilizers and pesticides.
Antibiotics Drugs such as penicillin, which kill bacteria and stop infections.
Arsenic A natural poison.
Artificial insemination A way of breeding animals which involves taking semen from a male animal, and implanting it into the womb of the female.
Bankrupt Unable to pay one's debts.
Biotechnology The exploitation of natural organisms.
Broiler A chicken bred for eating, sometimes kept in a 'broiler house'.
Cash crop A crop which is grown for sale to another country, rather than home consumption.
Cereal A plant which produces edible seeds, such as wheat or rice.
Cloning A way of producing identical copies of a plant, from just a few cells of the parent plant.
Commonwealth A group of countries throughout the world which were once British colonies.
Crop rotation A simple way of improving the soil, by growing different crops in it each year.
DDT A pesticide which is effective against many insects, but causes lasting damage to the environment.
Ecology The study of the relationships between living organisms and their environment.
Environment The surroundings and conditions in which we live.
Fascist A member of the anti-democratic political movement which began in Italy in the 1920s.
Fertility The ability of the soil to produce food, and of animals and plants to produce offspring.
Fertilizer Any substance used by farmers to improve the fertility of their soil and produce bigger harvests.
Free-range A natural way of keeping chickens in the open, rather than rearing them in cages in battery houses.
Granary A grain store.
Habitat The natural home of an animal or plant.
Herbicide A chemical which kills plants; selective herbicides can be used to kill weeds in food crops.
Hormone A substance which controls the growth of plants and animals.
Hybrid An animal or plant bred by crossing two different strains.
Hydroponic A soil-less way of growing plants by immersing their roots in nutrient solutions.

Industrial Revolution The transformation in the eighteenth and nineteenth centuries of many countries into industrial nations.
Insecticide A chemical which kills insects.
Irradiation The deliberate exposure of food and other materials to radioactivity, to preserve food.
Kibbutz (plural 'kibbutzim') A collective farm in Israel.
Leach To wash out of the soil.
Lime A calcium compound which is spread on the land to control acidity and improve the texture of the soil.
Malaria A disease spread by mosquitoes.
Meteorologist Someone who studies the world's weather patterns.
Microprocessor A small electronic circuit which acts as a computer.
Millet A cereal grass widely grown in Africa.
Organic Grown in a natural way, without using artificial chemicals.
Paddy Raw grains of rice, the rice plant, or the flooded field in which rice is grown.
Parasite An animal or plant which lives off another, such as the fleas and ticks found on farm animals.
Philosophy A system of ideas about the world, or the study of ideas.
Pneumatic Held up by air pressure, as with car tyres.
Protectionist A policy which supports a country's farmers, by giving them subsidies, or charging taxes on food from other countries.
Protein A nutrient which is essential for healthy growth in humans and animals.
Quota A limit on agricultural or industrial production.
Radioactive Emitting invisible particles, which can be dangerous to health.
Rationing A way of sharing out food supplies in times of shortage, by limiting each person to certain amounts of each food.
Selective breeding A way of improving animal and plant varieties by using only the best of each generation for breeding purposes.
Self-sufficient Able to produce enough food for one's needs without having to buy in stocks from elsewhere.
Share A part of a public company, which can be bought and sold on the stock market.
Sorghum A cereal cultivated for grain, hay and as a source of syrup.
Stock market The buying and selling of stocks and shares.
Subsidy A payment given to farmers when they grow certain crops.

Subsistence A way of farming which only just produces enough food for the farmer's needs, but no surplus for sale.
Threshing A process to remove the grain in cereal crops from the straw and husks.
Tuberculosis A disease which attacks the lungs.

U-boat An early German submarine, used in the First World War to attack shipping.
United Nations An organization of most of the world's countries, which meets to try to solve international problems.
Veal The flesh of young calves.

Further Reading

Alderson, Lawrence, **The Observer's Book of Farm Animals** (Frederick Warne 1978).
Barfield, Arnold, **Farming** (Wayland 1984).
Bolwell, Laurie and Lines, Clifford, **Farming the Land** (Wayland 1987).
Bolwell, Laurie and Lines, Clifford, **Farms and Farming** (Wayland 1984).
Bowman, Kenneth, **Visual Science: Agriculture** (Macdonald Educational 1985).
Hawkes, Nigel, **Farms** (Macdonald 1985).
Lambert, Mark, **The Future for the Environment** (Wayland, 1986).
Whitlock, Ralph, **Farming in History** (Wayland, 1982).
Wilkes, Peter, **An Illustrated History of Farming** (Spurbooks Ltd, 1978).

Picture acknowledgements
The illustrations in this book were supplied by: BBC Hulton Picture Library 8, 10, 11 (above), 12, 13 (both), 17; Bruce Coleman Ltd. (Mike Price) 4 (inset), (Hans Reinhard) 21, (Gordon Langsbury) 22 (above), (M. Timothy O'Keefe) 27, (Frans Lanting) 33 (above), (L.C. Marigo) 34 (left), 35, (Hans Reinhard) 36, (John Topham) 37, (Brian J. Coates) 38 (inset), 39 (inset); Camera Press 41 (below/inset); the Hutchison Library 20 (inset), 25, 26, 30 (above), 31, 41 (above); Mary Evans Picture Library cover/inset, 4 (main); The Mansell Collection 5 (below); Oxford Scientific Films Ltd. (Breck P. Kent) 5 (above), (D.H. Thompson) 23 (below), (Dr Nigel Smith) 29, (Peter Ward) 34 (right); Science Photo Library 42, 43, 44; TeleFocus 45; TOPHAM 6 (both), 11, 14 (inset), 15 (below), 16, 18, 22 (below), 23 (above), 24, 40, 41 (below/main); Zefa cover/main, 20 (main), 32, 38 (main); the remaining pictures are from the Wayland Picture Library.

Index

Acid rain 36, 37
Africa 5, 17
Agricultural Acts 12, 16
Agricultural Research Council, the 12
Agrigenetics 44
Argentina 6
Artificial insemination 9
Australia 4, 6, 10, 17, 23, 25, 32
Austria 10

'Battle for Wheat' 12
Belgium 24, 43
Biotechnology 42
Birdseye, Clarence 9
Brazil 10, 34
Britain 5, 6, 7, 12, 15, 23, 25, 34, 37

Chernobyl 37
China 40, 41
Cloning 42
Cloud Seeding 17
Collective Farming 13
Colombia 31
Colonial agriculture 4
Combine Harvesters 15, 19
Common Agricultural Policy (CAP) 25, 32
Common Customs Tariff 24
Computers 32, 44, 45
Cuba 10

DDT 18, 19
Deep-freezing 9
Denmark 6, 25
Depression, the 10
Developing world, the 28
Droughts 10, 28, 29, 31
'Dust Bowls' 10, 11, 32

Ecology Movement 33
Eire, the Republic of 25
Electric milking machines 9
Erosion 33, 34
Europe 5, 6, 7, 8, 9, 12, 20, 24, 37
European Economic Community (EEC) 24, 34, 40

Factory farming 20, 21, 37
Ferguson, Harry 9
Fertilizers 4, 9, 22, 29, 34, 38
First World War 7, 14
Fish farms 32, 39
Food and Agricuturre Organization (FAO) 19, 31
Ford, Henry 6
Forestry 32
Friends of the Earth 33

Genetic codes 42
Glasshouses 22, 26
Greece 25
Greenpeace 33
Green Revolution, the 26, 29, 31, 40

Hedgerows, destruction of 22, 34
Hormones 9, 21, 34
Hydroponic cultivation 26, 27

India 5, 29, 31, 40
Industrial Revolution 4
Insecticide 9, 18
Irradiation 42, 43
Italy 12, 24

Japan 10, 25, 32, 39

Kibbutz system 25

Land Army 7, 15
Landrace pig 22, 23
Live Aid 41
Luxembourg 24

Malnutrition 29
Müller, Paul 18
Mussolini, Benito 12, 13
Myxomatosis 23

New Deal, the 12
New Zealand 4, 6, 25
North America 4, 6, 8, 10, 12, 20, 25, 30, 32, 37, 38

Organic farming 36

Over-farming 10

Pakistan 29
Poland 10
Pollution 18, 37
Pontine marshes 12
Portugal 25
Prairies 6

Rain forests, destruction of 34, 35
Rationing 7, 14, 20
Refrigerated steamships 6
Rice 10, 15, 29, 30, 31, 38
Roosevelt. President 12
Russian Revolution 13

Sahara, the 34
Seaweed farming 39
Second World War 9, 14, 17, 18
Seed drill 6
Soya 26
Spain 25
Stalin 13
Subsidies 12, 16
Subsistence farming 28, 35

Tractors 9, 15, 16, 19
Treaty of Rome, the 24
Turkey 29

U-boats 7, 14
United Nations, the 19
USSR 37, 40

Veal 21

Wall Street Crash 10
Wallace, Henry 9
West Germany 24
West Indies 5